Terrorists Within Our Walls

The Principles of

Correctional Counterterrorism

Eric M. Vogt, CHS-V

ISBN-10: 1484162331
ISBN-13: 978-1484162330

DEDICATION

IN MEMORY OF F.B.I. SPECIAL AGENT JOHN O'NEILL, WHO
GAVE HIS CAREER AND HIS VERY LIFE ON
SEPTEMBER 11, 2001 TO PROTECT THE PUBLIC FROM
TERRORISM,

IN MEMORY OF MASSACHUSETTS INSTITUTE OF TECHNOLOGY
POLICE OFFICER SEAN COLLIER, WHO WAS SHOT AND KILLED
WHEN HE APPROACHED THE BOSTON MARATHON BOMBING
SUSPECTS ON APRIL 18, 2013,

–AND–

TO ALL OF THE DEDICATED MEN AND WOMEN WHO,
24 HOURS A DAY, SEVEN DAYS A WEEK PLACE THEMSELVES IN
HARM'S WAY TO PROTECT THE PUBLIC FROM CRIME AND
TERRORISM.

CONTENTS

"*I take this opportunity to address our prisoners, who are being held in Crusader jails, and especially our mujaheed Sheik Omar Abd Al-Rahman, as well as our prisoners in America... We have not forgotten you. We are still committed to the debt of your salvation. With Allah's strength, we will continue to deliver blows to America and its allies, until we shatter your shackles.*"

Ayman Al-Zawahiri, al-Qaida Leader

INTRODUCTION

The date was September 25, 1983. It was a quiet Sunday, much like any other weekend at Her Majesty's Prison Maze. But other quiet events had gone on in the months before. This was one of the prisons used to house members of the Provisional Irish Republican Army. These republican inmates were all clustered together by the prison administration to ensure peace with opposing factions. They had a highly organized violent extremist network. And they had a bold plan: Escape.

But the land around the prison was too muddy to tunnel through. And there were too many walls to scale. How could they do it? The plan unfolded clandestinely for months. Officers were watched. Patterns and procedures were noted. Those officers who were stricter drew many complaints from PIRA prisoners. As a result, administrators moved these officers to other posts.

The hat and uniform sizes of each officer on post were noted so that prisoners could use them. The PIRA prisoners learned much through their intelligence gathering on the corrections officers.

Sunday was ascertained to be the best day for the operation. Tea time left less staff to man critical security posts. Finally, all was ready to begin. The republicans then smuggled firearms into the institution.

Officers were overpowered; some were seriously injured. Over three dozen prisoners stuffed themselves into a truck and bolted for the vehicle gate. Shots rang out. A gate officer died instantly. Nineteen prisoners were captured at the gate. Nineteen others made it to freedom. A small band of them were never captured. It was the darkest day of the Northern Ireland Prison Service.

Many lessons were learned on that "quiet" day. Have you gleaned some of them already?

Today we do not face the exact same situation as the prisons in Northern Ireland faced. Yet, I wholeheartedly believe that the incarceration of violent extremist prisoners in the United States is one of the greatest challenges affecting civilian corrections today and in the future.

Long after their causes have waned, the worst of today's terrorists will remain in our civilian prison systems. It is the duty of each corrections worker, whether an officer or support staff, to be knowledgeable of and proficient in sound counterterrorism principles.

The idea for this handbook was rattling through my mind in the days leading up to my retirement from the United States Department of Justice, Federal Bureau of Prisons as an educator and law enforcement officer in 2011. My primary objective with this handbook is to prevent violent or criminal extremism in prisons by equipping the front line correctional worker with a basic understanding of these extremists and their methods. Since extremism often changes its form with time, I have tried to keep the information as general as possible to enable future corrections personnel with the ability to adapt the principles to their changing circumstances.

I use the terms "terrorist" and "violent or criminal extremist" interchangeably. For our purposes in corrections, these incarcerated individuals *advocate either violent or criminal actions to bring about political, social or religious change and take steps to execute or aid in the execution of such.* These individuals could act alone or be a member of an organized group. For the purposes of this book, this does not include criminal gangs.

I also use the term "he" in connection to individual terrorists for the sake of brevity. But anyone can be a terrorist regardless of gender, race, color, creed, ethnic persuasion, nationality or professed religion.

I was an instructor in counterterrorism for corrections and law enforcement officers in my local area of Missouri for about the last six years of my 27 year career in law enforcement. This gave me access to some of the most brilliant minds in the counterterrorism public service community. Everything I have laid out in this volume comes from their total experience. I have put the counterterrorism concepts into simple language and have adapted the principles for use specifically in a correctional environment.

I have offered this book as inexpensively as possible so that it can get the most extensive distribution it can to public servants involved with counterterrorism. I only ask the public and private agencies utilizing it to adhere to the same legal copyright restrictions that we all must adhere to. Pass the word to other professionals so they can procure this book for their front line personnel. And please remain vigilant for your own safety and the safety of your families, your community and your country.

Our prime objective in counterterrorism is to prevent violent or criminal extremist acts. Our second objective is to be ready to safely respond to a violent act of extremism. Our third objective is to be able to continue our operations after a terrorist event. I have focused on prevention in this volume because **I believe that we must be first Preventers, rather than first responders.** However, there is no golden bullet, no magic cure for the prevention of all terrorist acts. So we must be effective first responders as well.

I have purposefully used only open source information in compiling this volume. My personal experiences are offered in general terms as object lessons for the subject at hand so as to respect confidentiality issues.

The only facts I have revealed about extremists are the things that they themselves already know quite well. Take and adapt what you can to use in your respective environment and jurisdiction and within your own applicable guidelines, procedures, policies, regulations and statutes.

The incarceration of violent and criminal extremists is one of the greatest challenges facing corrections.

Long after their causes have waned, they will be in our correctional systems.

It is the duty of prison officers and support staff to be educated in correctional counterterrorism.

We must be first Preventers, rather than first responders.

Take what you can from these principles and adapt them to your jurisdictional procedures and statutes.

---

1 COUNTERTERRORISM AND CORRECTIONS

The extremist sat at his steel desk with a heavy lead pencil in his hand and a fire in his heart. He had been incarcerated for a number of months for a criminal offense. Most thought he was crazy. A few, and he, thought he was a hero of a righteous, almost holy struggle against injustice.

Yet he was relatively unknown. No one truly thought at the time of his incarceration that he would be historically significant in any global sense. But incarceration gave him the time and ability to ponder over his beliefs, to ingrain them into his heart and mind, to formulate them into words and to pen all down for members and future members of the movement.

Any prison worker who might have come across the extremist's manuscript likely would have found it highly illegible in its appearance. If he bothered to try to decipher the handwriting, he likely would have found the inmate's spelling and grammar atrocious, his ideas absurd and the content laboriously tedious to read. The official may have disregarded it as fiction or the writings of a deranged mind.

There is no official record that it was ever taken seriously by prison officials up until the day that he was released from the prison. At any rate, if a prison official did take it seriously, the information was apparently not documented and passed on to outside law enforcement so that the dealings of he and his violent extremist group could be monitored and its criminal activities prevented. If it had been, the extremist and his accomplices would have certainly been jailed for more stringent sentences for future plots.

This man was not a core al-Qaida operative or affiliate. Yet he brought about the deaths of some 55 million souls. His name was Adolph Hitler. The extremist writing he was formulating in prison was entitled *Mein Kampf*, or *"My Struggle"*. His violent extremist group was the National Socialist (Nazi) party.

We likely do not have a budding Adolph Hitler incarcerated at our facility. But we may have a very dangerous individual who, if left unsupervised to his or her own devices might contribute to or perpetrate himself a violent extremist act or other criminal act to further his cause.

Why is counterterrorism even an issue in U.S. correctional systems? We have seen regular terrorist activity inside the walls of Western prisons and even in American prisons in recent years.

In the United States, perhaps the most well-known case was of the Assembly of Authentic Islam (J.I.S.), the inmate radical Islamic militant group that recruited a prisoner in the New Folsom facility of the California prison system. About 6 months later he was released. He recruited more individuals at a Los Angeles area mosque and formed an attack cell. Their plan was to train themselves in small arms assault and to gather weapons purchased with the funds they stole through local gas station robberies.

These homegrown operatives sympathized with al-Qaida. The indictment indicates that they trained with firearms on a public firing range together. They also chose targets in the Los Angeles area that included U.S. Army recruiting stations, Israeli diplomats and the Israeli El Al airline counter in the terminal building of the Los Angeles LAX airport. If it weren't for a fluke, a cell phone dropped at the scene of a robbery, they may never have been discovered by law enforcement until it was too late. Fortunately the investigators involved with the robbery recognized the signs of a radicalized violent extremist group when conducting a search of an apartment they utilized.

In another recent case, a homegrown Islamic militant group that supported al-Qaida aims in Miami, Florida was indicted and pleaded guilty to a terrorism related conspiracy. The indictment states that two members had taken photographs of the Federal Detention Center in Miami. This group reportedly was also very interested in similar radicals who were incarcerated at the Metropolitan Correctional Center in Chicago, Illinois.

At the beginning of the war in Afghanistan, an al-Qaida affiliate's computer memory drive was found that contained the plans to the same U.S. prison where a popular Islamic violent extremist cleric and close friend of Osama bin Laden was incarcerated in the United States, prompting immediate around-the-clock security by special response teams.

While this same cleric was on trial earlier for a conspiracy to bomb New York landmarks, two letter bombs were sent from his group in their home country to a U.S. penitentiary and about 50 foreign tourists in his home country were slaughtered to protest his incarceration in America.

A young correctional officer at the Metropolitan Correctional Center in New York was severely brain damaged and almost killed by an al-Qaida operative who was trying to escape. His weapon? A sharpened comb.

While being held at the Federal Detention Center in Philadelphia, an Islamic militant who was part of a homegrown terrorist group that planned to conduct an armed assault on a military base reportedly even tried to proselytize to the judge presiding over the case!

Training manuals used by al-Qaida and its affiliates include instructions to their operatives on how to continue their operations if they are placed in prison. One training manual even tells operatives in detail how to attack a prison and a prisoner transport! And these types of attacks have been regularly perpetrated in Afghanistan, Pakistan, North Africa and elsewhere. The most notable was a recent explosives attack on a subway station that members of the Russian Security Service regularly use to commute to and from work at a facility that houses some of the most dangerous terrorist prisoners in their nation!

Another was a conspiracy uncovered in the British prison system where a militant inmate group planned to take an Islamic chaplain hostage and make a daring escape by helicopter! If it were not for an inmate informant, it may have been successful.

There are a few qualifiers I wish to emphasize before we go further:

1.   Not all inmates who advocate certain political, social or religious beliefs are necessarily violent or criminal extremists. The United States Constitution protects political and religious thought, belief and speech. But if an inmate commits or conspires to commit violence or other criminal acts to obtain these goals or their activity poses a danger to institutional security or public safety, that would warrant close monitoring and intervention.

2.   Extremism is not synonymous with criminal gang membership. However, extremists may commit criminal acts to further their extremist goal(s) of political, social or religious change. And extremists may be former gang members. They may also resemble a gang in behavior.

3. There should be several documented indicators before we identify an inmate as a violent or criminal extremist.
4. We are not concerned with religious belief or free speech protected by the Constitution.
5. Prejudice has no place in counterterrorism efforts. We are professionals.
6. We must be firm but fair in our dealings with all inmates. This directly contradicts al-Qaida and affiliate propaganda and aids in de-radicalization efforts. Remember that most American extremists will be released one day into the community----perhaps yours!

The prison environment lends itself to radicalization. Why do I say this? Criminals from various beliefs and backgrounds are brought together in close quarters, in most cases with the ability to associate and communicate with each other in open population. They are separated by some of the most influential people in their lives that would normally be a counterweight to radicalization, close friends and family, and they may be ostracized by those who are not radicals on the outside because of their criminal offense.

Inmates may be coming to prison with a set of perceived grievances against the government due to their incarceration or criminal experiences. In addition, they have nothing but time to ponder over personal grievances and the spectrum of different belief systems, both beneficial and radical, while they are incarcerated. Because some extremists are convicted of criminal statutes and not terrorism-related statutes, correctional staff may not even be immediately alerted to their potential to be a radicalization influence on other inmates. These extremists may have time to influence other inmates to adopt similar beliefs before they are detected.

Inmates in both open population and closed population will communicate and associate with each other in any way possible. It could be face-to-face. But it may be by smuggled note, by verbal communication through walls or air ducts. It may be by visits from family members or others, contraband personal letters, contraband legal mail, illicit or authorized phone conversations, e-mails, extremist publications and other extremist media.

Does this mean that all who associate with an extremist will be radicalized? Not necessarily. Before radicalization, the inmate may be searching through many different belief systems of other inmates and outside groups, extremist and non-extremist. This search or experimentation is not sufficient to indicate a need for close monitoring. Indeed, the sheer number of inmates who are searching in this manner makes it impossible for prison staff to closely monitor them all in an open prison population.

There should be several pieces of documented evidence of radicalization before an inmate is designated one who will be closely monitored. The exception to this is when there is <u>any</u> evidence of training in or planning of violent acts of extremism or of close association or affiliation with illicit terrorist organizations. We will further discuss the dynamics of extremist radicalization and organization in later chapters.

This brings up the question: How should we respond when we detect evidence of violent or criminal extremism?

It depends on the circumstances. If an imminent act of violence is expected to occur then common sense dictates immediate intervention, the segregating of the involved individuals from other inmates to prevent the violence and the confiscation of any evidence or contraband. However, if this is not the case, many times it is better to more closely monitor the individual(s) to determine the extent of the activity. This may lead to very valuable intelligence gathering and analysis or to indicators of further criminal conspiracy. It may yield more evidence in time that can aid in the criminal prosecution of all of the conspirators. Once again, this is a professional judgment call that the authorized law enforcement or correctional official must live with. Remember that life safety and institutional security comes first. If evidence of an imminent violent act or an imminent escape attempt is uncovered, a quick response may be warranted.

Investigative and intelligence staff may gather and glean much valuable information. But many times it is the front line correctional employee, the one who has frequent contact with inmates, that has the most chance of discovering a violent or criminal extremist individual or group.

Remember that it was not the Federal Bureau of Investigation who pulled over Timothy McVeigh, the Oklahoma City bomber, in a routine traffic stop. It was not the Bureau of Alcohol, Tobacco, Firearms and Explosives that noted something out of the ordinary which led to his arrest. It was a front line state law enforcement officer who noted McVeigh's suspicious behavior and found enough evidence of criminal activity to arrest him while fleeing the scene of the bombing. When federal agents finally identified him as a person of interest in the bombing, they found him in jail.

In much the same way, the front line corrections employee, whether an officer or a support staff member, is likely the one who will first start noting irregularities in inmate dress, grooming or behavior. Investigative, intelligence or front line staff may receive information from an inmate informant. For this reason, *it is imperative that ALL corrections front line employees, whether officers or support staff, be regularly and proficiently trained* in the skills outlined in this handbook. They should also be trained to recognize and immediately pass on intelligence information as it is noted, no matter how minor it may seem, both verbally and in writing to the appropriate supervisory, intelligence and investigative personnel.

The issue of violent and criminal extremist activity in prison is a serious one for correctional staff all around the world. To believe that the United States is immune to these activities is unreasonable. Let us not commit the same error that the highest administrators did in the Federal Bureau of Investigation and other federal agencies when Special Agent John O'Neill adamantly warned of the threat of a new international organization called al-Qaida. This ostrich-like attitude of some federal, state and local officials toward terrorism ended in the greatest cataclysm on American soil since Pearl Harbor on September 11, 2001.

We must be proactive. We must remain alert. We must be well trained. We must be ready. We must continuously reassess the threats from violent or criminal extremists in prisons.

In the next chapter we will examine the principles of anti-terrorism security by looking from the inside of the prison outward.

> **The front line prison employee, whether an officer or support staff, is the person most likely to detect signs of violent or criminal extremism.**
>
> **We must be proactive in counterterrorism.**
>
> **We must be well-trained and remain alert to signs of terrorism.**

2 COUNTERTERRORISM SECURITY FROM THE INSIDE LOOKING OUT

> **"GATHER INFORMATION USING ALL AVAILABLE MEANS...FORMER PRISONERS, PEOPLE WHO WORKED IN THE PRISON...OR PEOPLE WHO VISITED THERE..."**
>
> *HOW TO STORM A PRISON*

In order to keep the institution and the public safe from violent extremism, we must first look at the institution from the inside of the prison outward. In the past, this was done to restrict unauthorized communications, introduction of contraband and escapes. With the advent of terrorism, however, the focus must include the prevention of violent and criminal extremism.

In Europe, North Africa, the Middle East and South Asia, violent extremist organizations have staged attacks on and/or terrorist escapes from jails and prisons. These groups consider their incarcerated brothers as prisoners of war. These incarcerated individuals are mentioned frequently in propaganda released by their terrorist organizations.

A general principle of anti-terrorism defense at hard targets that has been used in Israel and other Middle Eastern nations with effectiveness is the utilization of several layers of security. The goal is to either stop or slow down an intruder from entering the target. This includes fences, barricades, walls, armed and barricaded towers, armed mobile personnel, secure access points with armed personnel and an effective threat based intelligence operation.

If one layer is attacked or breached, the other layers are notified. The mobile personnel can be held in reserve and dispatched to support penetrated areas. Extra layers can be designated and manned as alert levels heighten in a homeland security crisis. Routine mobile unit personnel should be thoroughly trained in these procedures and be equipped with the necessary weapons and equipment to respond to a terrorist incident.

Procedures should be adequately outlined by emergency plans and all staff regularly trained in their implementation. Regular desktop and physical exercises should be performed that include active involvement of local first responders.

The goals of full scale exercises are to give prison employees hands-on and realistic training and to ascertain if the emergency procedures need modification. They also build rapport with other first response agencies. Memorandums of Understanding should be in writing and agreed to by each agency's person in authority in advance. They should clearly delineate what local first responding agencies will do and the specific resources they will do it with to support the correctional facility in a terrorist incident. The incident command system should be utilized to enable coordination between the different agencies involved in a future homeland security event.

When we in the civilian correctional sphere are speaking about layers of security, we must also include the outermost layer of security: criminal extremist intelligence gathering, analysis and dissemination. If there are adequate information sharing systems in place with local, state and federal government agencies, this can be the most effective way to actually prevent a terrorism incident from occurring before it happens.

Entry Screening

Entry screening is familiar to most correctional employees who enter and exit the prison each day. Your correctional facility likely already has sound policies relating to the entry of inmate visitors and official visitors in an effort to keep unauthorized personnel off of the property, to prevent the introduction of contraband and prevent escapes. In the area of counterterrorism, however, there are certain points that should be considered.

First of all, when terrorists are mentioned, a picture may come to mind of someone like Timothy McVeigh or Osama bin Laden. We may have a stereotypical view of what a terrorist looks like, but this is a dangerous view for a corrections professional to take.

What it comes down to is: anyone could be a terrorist. Terrorists can be young or old, male or female, of any race or nationality. Trained terrorists know the value of deception and of blending into their surroundings. Terrorists can even be fellow staff members, contractors or volunteers!

Radical Islamic terrorist groups have realized the value of using females in operations. They have found that security forces tend to let down their guard with females. We have seen more and more use of females in attacks.

Terrorists make good use of fraudulent identification. Check out photo identification thoroughly. Ask detailed questions. Some groups like al-Qaida have stolen uniforms, official vehicles in use at target facilities and emergency or police vehicles so that they can get close enough to attack and suddenly overwhelm unsuspecting checkpoint personnel. Never assume that a person is who he/she appears to be.

Terrorists are also human. They can get nervous during operations. Watch for increased perspiration, rapid breathing and nervous eye and limb movement as you are questioning visitors. Also watch for signs of being under the influence of drugs, since suicide bombers in Middle Eastern lands have been known to take drugs before an operation.

Look at the visitor's clothing. Is he/she dressed according to the weather? Or is the visitor wearing a coat or several layers of clothing in mild weather that may be capable of hiding a bomb vest? Are his/her hands free or are they grasping something? Do you see any wiring? Remember that suicide vests can be worn by any member of a terrorist team as a last resort to kill checkpoint personnel and to ensure that the operative is not captured. Instructions to a suicide bomber are: if you are discovered before getting to the target, detonate the charges in place. If you suspect a suicide bomber, you may have just a brief moment to protect yourself and those around you before detonation. Center mass should not be targeted when using firearms against suicide bombers. This could detonate a suicide vest, with disastrous effects for you and any bystanders.

Sometimes terrorists will probe a target to test the security apparatus before an attack actually occurs. Some groups even perform "dry runs", or dress rehearsals, without weapons or bombs, of their operations before an actual attack. Any unauthorized person attempting to enter a checkpoint should be thoroughly investigated and the incident documented, no matter how minor or innocent it may seem. Terrorist groups often do reconnaissance before an operation, using cameras, camcorders and cell camcorders. Any persons with such devices must be thoroughly investigated. If these individuals are off property, the shift supervisor should be contacted so that local law enforcement can investigate. Camcorders are also commonly used by terrorists to record the attack. In the case of a suicide bomber, a "handler" will frequently escort him to the vicinity of the target to ensure that the attack takes place. Be alert for other terrorists in the immediate area. Remember that even volunteers, contractors and employees could be terrorists who have infiltrated the institution. They can also be corrupted or manipulated into introducing contraband such as weapons, cell phones, etc.

Never allow a visitor who has not been thoroughly searched to use a restroom in the facility and never allow them to approach or manipulate barricades, flower vases landscaping or garbage receptacles, as a bomb could easily be hidden for future detonation.

In the next chapter we will delve more deeply into counterterrorism readiness.

Utilize multiple layers of security.

Have an effective intelligence system.

Remember that <u>Anyone</u> could be a terrorist.

Be alert for suspicious behavior and dress.

Assess counterterrorism needs regularly.

Prepare and regularly update contingency plans.

Conduct counterterrorism training with <u>ALL</u> employees.

Conduct tabletop and realistic full scale exercises with local responders, reassess needs afterward and update your plans and training.

3 COUNTERTERRORISM SECURITY READINESS

Terrorism Threat Assessments

A detailed threat assessment for terrorism related risk should be routinely completed of the facility to determine high risk assets in order of importance. This assessment is used to allocate limited funding to more security for the highest at-risk areas. Assessments should be done regularly, because circumstances and terrorist threats can change quickly.

Contingency Planning and Training

Contingency plans should be written that detail layered security to be employed in case of different threat levels, as determined by the Chief Executive Officer. But making written response guidelines without appropriate staff training is a dangerous mixture. First responder staff should be thoroughly trained in the implementation of these plans and in the incident command system. Exercises that stress unified command with local law enforcement and emergency response personnel should be emphasized and memorandums of understanding should be employed by the cooperating agencies so that the agencies are familiar with response procedures prior to an emergency occurring.

A common mistake made with contingency planning training is that often management and special response teams are routinely trained while the potential first responders, front line staff, receive little or no training. Experience has shown that <u>a terrorist attack must have an effective response in the first minutes to properly contain the incident</u> and to mitigate the effects of such an attack. First responder training is therefore critical to effective anti-terrorism measures at the institutional level.

Training should be hands-on and realistic. Its purpose should be to reveal the need for changes in contingency planning and procedures. This is a continuous, on-going process.

<u>Contingency plans should be practical</u> and commensurate with actual resources at hand and realistic security capabilities. They should be tailored specifically for the individual institution's terrorism response needs. They should state procedures to put into place for each homeland security threat level. <u>The incident command system should be utilized</u> in contingency plans. They should be as detailed as possible but allow enough flexibility for the incident commander and operations section chief to respond effectively to changing circumstances.

What lessons did the Katrina hurricane response have for contingency planners? One is that a detailed chain-of-command structure utilizing both the incident command and unified command models must be addressed in any contingency planning. <u>Realistic exercises should be held regularly</u> that include all agencies that could possibly be involved in a variety of scenarios.

Memorandums of understanding should be made with other agencies <u>outside</u> of those in the immediate local area so that if local resources are overwhelmed by a common disaster or have been diverted to other concurrent incidents, resources can be quickly tapped from non-local entities. Most of all, *meaningful* training in the implementation of emergency plans should be held regularly with <u>all</u> potential first responders. Continuity of operations training specific to the institution should also be included in a training program.

The general elements of an effective first response include making an initial assessment of the incident, containment and control of the incident, resource allocation for the first and continuing response, mitigation of the effects of the incident and return to normal operations as soon as possible. As changes occur during and after the initial response, the incident command system outlined in the contingency plans should be able to cope with the challenges of command structure, strategic and tactical planning and implementation, procurement, allocation and reimbursement of resources, the gathering, analysis and dissemination of information, accountability of staff procedures and end-of-incident procedures.

Contingency plans should be constantly updated and input encouraged from all staff, whether investigative, intelligence, training or response when reviewing contingency plans.

ALL POTENTIAL FIRST RESPONDERS SHOULD RECEIVE REGULAR, MEANINGFUL TRAINING IN CONTINGENCY PLANS AND TERRORISM INCIDENT PROCEDURES.

CONTINGENCY PLANS SHOULD BE REALISTIC AND COMMENSURATE WITH ACTUAL RESOURCES AT HAND.

THE INCIDENT COMMAND SYSTEM SHOULD BE UTILIZED AND INCLUDED IN CONTINGENCY PLANS.

THERE SHOULD BE COORDINATION BETWEEN INTELLIGENCE, INVESTIGATIVE, TRAINING AND FRONT LINE EMERGENCY RESPONSE PERSONNEL WHEN CONTINGENCY PLANS ARE REVIEWED AND UPDATED.

---

4 CHARACTERISTICS OF INTERNATIONAL VIOLENT EXTREMISTS

"The brother should not accept any work that may belittle or demean him or his brothers, such as the cleaning of the prison bathrooms or hallways."

"The brothers should create an Islamic program for themselves inside the prison, as well as recreational and educational ones, etc."

"Brothers should also pay attention to each other's needs and should help each other and unite (against and/or corrupt) the prison officers..."

Al Qaeda Manual

The term "terrorism" comes from the 14th century French word *terreur*, used to describe the time of the French revolution, when arbitrary law and the guillotine reigned, instilling terror into the local populous. Terrorism is a difficult term to define, since there is no universal agreement in the United Nations as to what the definition of terrorism is. One nation's "terrorist" is another nation's "freedom fighter". The Federal Bureau of Investigation's definition of terrorism is:

"The unlawful use of force against persons or property to intimidate or coerce a government, the civilian population, or any segment thereof, in the furtherance of political or social objectives."

Terrorism has been around since ancient times, but modern Islamic radical militancy and some other forms of modern world terrorism can be traced to the end of the brutality of World War I. Colonial powers of Europe were locked in a bloody struggle for over four years. Advances in the warfare technology made the tactics of the Napoleonic era outdated and resulted in some 9 million deaths on the battlefield. Royal lines and kingdoms were swept away and those that survived struggled to hold on to their colonial possessions. One of the areas affected was the Middle East.

When the Ottoman Empire (present day Turkey) declared war on the British Empire, Britain proceeded to occupy areas of present day Egypt and the Middle East. In order to obtain an ally against the Turks, British officials promised Arab nomadic tribal leaders that if they united against their Turkish rulers, they would be given their freedom from both European and Turkish colonial rule. These Arab leaders united and with the aid of British weaponry pushed Turkish forces out of occupied Arab lands, eventually taking Damascus. But, unknown to the Arabs, the British and French had forged an agreement to partition the Middle East after the war. Despite Arab and American opposition, this was imposed by the Treaty of Versailles and the two states of the Trans-Jordan and Iraq would eventually be formed. All other Middle-Eastern areas would remain under direct French and British oversight. This brought with it an Arab distrust of European powers and a feeling of betrayal to the Arab world.

This feeling of betrayal would be enhanced by the League of Nations mandate authorizing a British protectorate in Palestine and the subsequent U.N. general assembly authorization of a Jewish partition in 1947. The declaration of the state of Israel in 1948 brought war to the region. The Israelis won their war of independence at great cost to both sides. Some 700,000 Arab Palestinians were displaced from their homes to refugee camps in Lebanon, Syria and Jordan. About 10,000 were killed and 30,000 wounded. The refugees would not be allowed by Israel to return.

In 1967, Egypt, Iraq, Syria, Jordan and other Islamic states prepared for a war to annihilate Israel. In an effort to preempt this attack, Israeli forces attacked first the Egyptian and then the Jordanian air forces, completely destroying them and preventing the Arab states and their allies from launching a successful ground assault.

In 1973, the Arab states and Egypt launched a sneak attack on the Jewish holiday of Yom Kippur and appeared to be ready to defeat the Israelis. The United States supported the Israelis with weapons and economic aid and the attack was repelled at great human cost.

Arabs felt that the U.S. had betrayed them just as the Europeans had done. They launched an oil embargo of the U.S., the beginning of a united Arab economic strategy that reaches to the present day. Today Israel is over double its original size in 1948. Although peace has been made with Egypt and Jordan, disputes over land ownership continue to deride peace talks with the Palestinians and Syria.

Where does modern Islamic radicalism fit into this history? In the 7th & 8th centuries, successors of the Prophet Mohammed had spread the Islamic empire to present day Pakistan in the east and present day Spain and Morocco in the west. Spice trading had extended the reach of Islamic merchants and their religion as far away as present day Malaysia, Indonesia and the Philippines. The Islamic caliphate was a military and scientific power superior to European civilization for hundreds of years.

After the fall of the Islamic caliphate and the eventual dominance of European powers, Muslim scholars searched for explanations of the Islamic decline. Their explanations would center on the perceived failure of Muslims in general to adhere to certain fundamentalist beliefs of the teachings of the Prophet Mohammed. An 18th century imam, al Wahhab, would produce a sect that would again rise in influence at the time of World War I to dominate Sunni Islamic thought in the Arab world: Wahhabism (called Salafism today by its adherents). The Wahhabis included imams who taught the idea of a return to fundamentalist beliefs of the first three generations of Mohammed's followers. They supported the house of Saud's rule over the Arabian Peninsula in the early 20th century and became the state-approved religion there. It was exported to other Muslim states.

In Egypt, in 1928, the inequities of British colonial rule were opposed by Hassan al Banna, a schoolteacher who was influenced by Wahhabism. He formed the Muslim Brotherhood. The Muslim Brotherhood's original intent was to non-violently oppose secular rulers they viewed as corrupt and vie for social change. They developed an international influence through branch offices that reached as far as the United States. In Egypt the Muslim Brotherhood was put down violently, with members tortured in prisons and killed. Some secret militant groups sprang from the Muslim Brotherhood movement.

During the Cold War, Marxist-based pan-Arab ideas and groups sprang up across the Muslim world, resulting in secular governments being established in Egypt, Syria, Libya, Yemen, Iraq and elsewhere. The ruling kingdoms in Saudi Arabia and Jordan remained. The Muslim Brotherhood would counter these governments, seeking social reform. Some former Muslim Brotherhood adherents, including Sayyad Qutb (executed by Nasser in Egypt in 1966), felt that even more violent means were justified to fight secular rulers.

This concept was further extended by offshoot groups, to include Abdullah Azzam's M.A.K. (Office of Services for the Mujahideen), becoming a God-supported conflict between the *umma* (the worldwide association of faithful Muslims) and the *kufr* (those who do not practice true Islam). They felt that a return to a form of Islam based on the strict fundamentalist interpretation of their faith would result in Allah's (God's) blessing upon Islamic peoples and the eventual restoration of the caliphate. The M.A.K. (and later al-Qaida) would use the framework of the worldwide Muslim Brotherhood organization to its own ends in this struggle.

Before the decline of the Cold War, the minority Shiite Islamic leaders saw their goal of a religious government take place with the ousting of the Shah of Iran and the rise of Ayatollah Khomeini in February 1979. In December 1979 the Soviet Union invaded neighboring Afghanistan to prevent a similar religious government there. Pakistan encouraged Arab fighters to come to its country to train and then enter Afghanistan to fight. This resulted in dozens of *mujahideen* (holy warriors) training bases being set up on both sides of the Afghani-Pakistani border. Saudi Arabia, private donors and the United States funneled billions of dollars through the Pakistani I.S.I. (Directorate for Inter-services Intelligence) to these groups.

One of these groups was led by Abdullah Azzam, a Palestinian Islamic theologian who believed in a pan-Arab Islamic state. He believed that the first fight for this state would be in Afghanistan, and that Muslims throughout the world had to unite and aid the Afghani Muslims in any way possible to defeat the Soviets and their proxy government. He formed the M.A.K., an organization to aid in the recruitment and financing of radical Islamic Arab fighters.

Offices for this group sprang up all over the world, generally following the framework of the Muslim Brotherhood organization. It raised money as far away as the United States. Osama bin Laden, who was a former university student of Azzam's, supported the M.A.K. with money, supplies and his own hard work. He would become embroiled in what he saw as a conflict between not only the Afghans and the Soviet Union, but between Muslims and non-Muslims worldwide. When Azzam was assassinated in 1989, Osama bin Laden, with the support of radical Islamic spiritual leader Sheik Omar Abdel Rahman and physician Ayman al-Zawahiri, assumed leadership over the structure of M.A.K. and eventually transformed it into the organization known today as al-Qaida (literally "the base").

Core al-Qaida prior to September 11th had, at its peak, 100-200 "hardcore" members who networked with perhaps hundreds of Islamic associates of the Soviet-Afghan War. Today only a handful of these original hardcore members remain alive and outside custody. They have to remain in deep hiding or they will be targeted by the United States and its allies.

Today, with the resurgence of core al-Qaida, there are once again some 100 hard core operatives, operating out of the tribal areas in northwest Pakistan.

What is generally (incorrectly) referred to as "al-Qaida" today by the press and governments? The Soviet-Afghan War associates of core al-Qaida and other organized Sunni radical Islamic sub-groups (including small, unconnected homegrown cells relying on internet recruitment and training) that have adopted some (but not necessarily all) of the goals and/or tactics of core al-Qaida. These sub-groups are actually part of a broad-based radical Islamic militant movement that is struggling against Israel, the West and the secular governments of the Muslim world. This modern day "al-Qaida" is not a well-structured, worldwide organization. It is a loose alliance of local internationalist sub-groups of the broad-based radical Islamic movement. In this way we could term the modern day al-Qaida as more of a movement than a single group.

These new al-Qaida "franchises" or sub-groups cooperate with one another when it coincides with their local and worldwide goals. Normally, these groups could be in competition, if not at out-and-out war with one another. Yet, they are cooperative with one another when it is in the best interest of their local struggle due to their common enemies.

Core al-Qaida

Perhaps the most well-known terrorist group today because of its links to the attacks of September 11th, core al-Qaida actually had a vague, secretive history prior to those attacks. The term al-Qaida (also frequently spelled al-Qaeda– the transliteration of Arabic into English is not an exact science and either spelling is correct) actually means "the base". It also has a variety of other meanings including "the foundation" and "the method".

Followers of al-Qaida consider themselves to be the elite vanguard of the radical Islamic militancy movement. They believe that by their zealous terrorist acts they can incite other Muslims to join this movement. Before his death, followers generally swore a *bayat* (oath of allegiance) to their spiritual leader Osama bin Laden, although not all were required to do so.

Al-Qaida was likely formed at the beginning of the 1990's. The 1993 World Trade Center bombing was perpetrated by Ramzi Yousef, nephew and associate of Khalid Sheik Mohammed, mastermind of 9/11. Yousef recruited his co-conspirators from a radical mosque which hosted Sheik Omar Abdel Rahman. Rahman was later connected to the first World Trade Center bombing as well as conspiring to a series of subsequent attacks on New York landmarks. Attacks on the two U.S. embassies in Kenya and Tanzania and on the U.S.S. Cole were perpetrated by al-Qaida associates prior to 9/11. After 9/11, Richard Reid, the "shoe bomber" attempted to destroy a plane flying from Paris to the United States.

M.A.K. was a forerunner of the al-Qaida network. While M.A.K. originally supported the Afghani conflict against the Soviets, al-Qaida used the MAK international organization to support its worldwide jihad effort. Al-Qaida aided any like-minded radical Islamic militant groups as long as they supported its interests. Different individuals and groups would approach bin Laden's leadership circle requesting aid for specific plans of attack. If approved by the leadership, the sub-group would receive money, equipment, training and/or personnel in aid.

The multi-million dollar funds used by al-Qaida were administered through an elaborate network of financial fronts such as charities and corporate businesses. These followed the long-used Muslim Brotherhood's model of hiding funds from authorities. Al-Qaida used multiple front organizations in a "shell game" of passing money to and from the different organizations, eventually funneling the money to specific terrorist operations.

To adherents of al-Qaida and other radical Islamic militant groups, the Soviet Union was defeated in Afghanistan and subsequently disintegrated solely due to the will of Allah, or God. By adhering to fundamentalist beliefs and joining the universal God-supported war against unbelievers, al-Qaida members are assured, if they die, of a heavenly reward in paradise conditions. To them, this is a jihad, or armed struggle, that will continue until the caliphate is restored to Muslim lands. They feel that, just as the Soviet Union fell, Allah will destroy the United States, Western allies, and secular Arab, North African and Asian governments and Islam will again be ascendant in the world.

Al-Qaida operatives are organized along the "cell" format of the World War II French resistance and the Soviet bloc intelligence cells. Only the leader, or commander of the cell has any contact with anyone of the organization outside of the cell. Each cell member is trained for a specific function. Prior to an attack operatives will do thorough intelligence gathering and reconnaissance of the target, many times photographing, cell cam recording or videotaping the target. Probing of target security and dry runs, or dress rehearsals, of the attack plan may be completed prior to the actual attack. Generally, core al-Qaida operatives plan so thoroughly that they are 100% convinced they will succeed . They may also videotape or cell cam record the actual attack for propaganda purposes. Documents and videotapes seized in Afghanistan indicate that Al-Qaida has procured and tested chemical weapons and has attempted to procure biological weapons.

Hezbollah

Before September 11th, Hezbollah ("Party of God", also known as Lebanese Islamic Jihad) held the distinction of being the #1 killer of U.S. citizens amongst Islamic terrorist groups. A Lebanese Shi'a group, Hezbollah is deeply affiliated with the Iranian and Syrian governments. Its political arm is now a powerful part of the Lebanese government. It arose in response to the 1982 Israeli invasion of southern Lebanon. In 1983 it was responsible for the bombings of both the U.S. embassy and the U.S. Marine barracks in Beirut. It was also responsible for the kidnap and torture-killing of a U.S. Marine colonel and a C.I.A. section chief, in addition to kidnapping about 30 other Westerners. In 1984 the bombing of the U.S. Embassy annex in Beirut resulted in the withdrawal of the U.S. from Lebanon. A U.S. Navy Seal was murdered by Hezbollah operatives in a 1985 plane hijacking.

Hezbollah financial cells have existed for many years in the U.S. and South America. Hezbollah terror cells in the tri-border region of South America are blamed for the bombing of the Israeli embassy and a Jewish cultural center in Buenos Aires in the mid-1990's.

Hezbollah has been called a greater threat to U.S. interests than al-Qaida by some intelligence analysts because of its more advanced organization in the Americas and because of its link to the Iranian intelligence services.

Hezbollah financial cells have been found in the eastern and northern U.S. and there has been at least one case of a Hezbollah-backed immigration ring on the Mexican border that has smuggled Middle-Easterners into the United States.

Hezbollah was instrumental in training Palestinian Hamas operatives in suicide bombing techniques that have targeted Israel since April 1993.

Hamas

Hamas is an offshoot of the pan-Arab Muslim Brotherhood movement. It was formed in 1987. It is opposed to the existence of Israel and denies the legitimacy of the 1993 Oslo Accords. It teaches that jihad is needed to wrestle control of Palestine from Israeli hands and is a necessary duty of all Palestinians. It has been involved in suicide bombings since April of 1993. It is a rival of the secular Fatah movement, which it considers as corrupt, and controls Gaza. Hamas' civilian wing has provided Palestinians with hospitals, schools and other social services, making them extremely popular and winning them a majority of seats in the Palestinian government in 2006, prior to the West Bank-Gaza split.

Hamas reportedly has links to both Hezbollah and the Iranian government, which it receives some funding from. It has had financial cells in the United States and was involved in fund raising through the HLF charitable organization until its assets were frozen by the U.S. government. Wadih Al Hage's personal phone/address book, seized by U.S. agents in Kenya, indicate that al-Qaida may have been involved in Hamas' money laundering through the HLF charity in the 1990's, but this connection is not conclusive. Although rivals for membership, Hamas also has links to the Palestinian Islamic Jihad and reportedly has cooperated with them in some money laundering operations in the U.S.

In 1997, Palestinian men with loose links to Hamas members were found by NYPD officers with improvised explosive devices in a Brooklyn apartment. These men apparently intended to commit a suicide bombing of a New York City subway line that was used heavily by Jewish business people.

Palestinian Islamic Jihad

Palestinian Islamic Jihad is far smaller than Hamas and lacks its social network. It was started in 1974 as a West Bank extension of Egyptian Islamic Jihad. PIJ has used women and teens as suicide bombers against Israel. A suicide attack on an Israeli restaurant in Tel Aviv on April 17, 2006 was attributed to PIJ. Nine bystanders were killed. Both PIJ and Hamas spokesmen stated that it was a legitimate attack of Palestinian resistance. Palestinian Islamic Jihad's financial backing is thought to be from Iran and Syria.

5 CHARACTERISTICS OF DOMESTIC VIOLENT AND CRIMINAL EXTREMISTS

This is a brief general summary of the evolution of the far-right movement in the United States which resulted in the rise of some splinter violent or criminal extremist lone wolves and groups.

We must remember that <u>most</u> far right groups are protected by the Constitutional right of free speech and/or freedom of religion. We are not concerned with these far right groups, which seek political change through non-violent or non-criminal means. **We are concerned with only those individuals or groups that use violent or criminal means to attempt to achieve their aims.**

This is not a question of politics. Remember that far left violent criminal extremists could be just as dangerous as far right extremist militants to law enforcement officers. Because most deaths and injuries by domestic extremist acts in the United States have been committed by right wing violent or criminal extremists, we have included a summary of the history of this movement below.

Generally, those who resort to domestic terrorism to achieve their goals of political, social and/or religious change share one common enemy, whether of one side of the extreme or the other: they deny the authority of and oppose the government of the United States. In some cases, though their political goals are on opposite ends of the spectrum, adherents of these groups have praised each other's efforts against government authority on social media.

The American Neo-Nazi and Radical Right Violent or Criminal Movements

German authorities imprisoned Adolph Hitler in 1924, where he wrote his political manifesto entitled *Mein Kampf*, or "My Struggle" Upon release the German National Socialist Party gained popularity. Hitler was appointed as chancellor of Germany in 1933. Upon attaining dictatorial powers by blaming the Reichstag fire on the communists, Hitler and the Nazi Party commenced a national demonizing of the Jews. Those who dissented with the regime were imprisoned in concentration camps. With the Nazi invasion of Poland in 1939 came the Second World War. In 1942 "The Final Solution", the mass deportation of Jews in occupied territories, began. It is estimated that 6 million Jews died in what came to be called the Holocaust. The 3rd Reich fell in 1945.

When the United States entered the war, the U.S. government began the internment of German nationals in detainment camps. Crystal City, Texas was one such camp. At the beginning of internment the percentage of Nazis in this camp was estimated to be just 10% of all of the German detainees. These 10% had, by the end of the war, radicalized almost the entire remaining 90% of detainees as Nazis. At the end of World War II in 1945, American authorities determined that the detainees at Crystal City had become so radicalized that most could not be released in the United States. Those up for deportation were placed on Ellis Island until their status was settled. The last detainees would not be released until 1948, about three full years after the war's end.

In the following years the U.S. became embroiled in the Cold War against the Communist bloc of nations. Senator Joseph McCarthy started his campaign against U.S. citizens alleged to be communists.

George Lincoln Rockwell, a U.S. Naval veteran of World War II, determined that communists were the true enemy, not Hitler. He converted to Nazism and became the leader of the post-war American Nazi Party. Rockwell became known as "The Great Advertiser" of neo-Nazism. He started an Anti-Civil Rights Movement. The American Nazi Party coined slogans such as "We will save the white race!" and "White Power!" Jews, Blacks, Gays, and Catholics were hailed as enemies. In 1966 these neo-Nazis staged a counter-demonstration to Martin Luther King's protest in Chicago. Then came Rockwell's assassination.

William Pierce agreed with Rockwell's message of American Neo-Nazism. He felt that there was enormous Jewish influence upon American media. He became the founder of the National Alliance. Pierce would write a novel depicting a Neo-Nazi revolution set in the future called *The Turner Diaries*. It became a blueprint for murder and was hailed as the new "Bible" of the right wing radical militant movement.

In the 1980's neo-Nazis would go from talk to action: The small neo-Nazi group called "The Order" was founded by Robert Mathews, David Lane and Bruce Pierce. This terrorist cell committed armored car robberies to fund their extremist attacks. They assassinated Alan Berg, a Jewish radio talk show host in Denver who took a vocal stand against the neo-Nazi movement. A manhunt for members of The Order ended with Mathews' death in their firefight with law enforcement on Whidbrey Island. Bruce Pierce would die at FCC Allenwood of natural causes on August 16, 2010.

Richard Butler founded a neo-Nazi group called The Aryan Nations. After the Ruby Ridge standoff and Waco Standoff a young veteran named Timothy McVeigh hardened his stance against the federal government. He and two others gathered the makings of an ammonium nitrate bomb. The result was the Oklahoma City bombing of the Murrah Federal Building. This attack mimicked the scenario depicted in *The Turner Diaries* where a Neo-Nazi freedom fighter parked a vehicle with an explosive device in the underground parking garage of the F.B.I. Headquarters in Washington, DC, completely destroying the building.

Richard Butler felt that the internet was "the one thing that the Jews cannot control." The use of the internet spurred on the radical right militant movement, including adherents of the Christian Identity religion, Freemen, Common Law, Sovereign Citizen, National Socialist Movement and Militia movements. This mass communication resulted in increased membership. There were sporadic incidents of individual or group intimidation of government officials and others who opposed their views and spurred on hate crimes.

In West Memphis, Arkansas, two Sovereign Citizens surprised officers with assault weapons when their car was stopped by police for a traffic violation. The two police officers were killed and two more wounded in the ensuing chase and firefight.

Both Timothy McVeigh and Eric Rudolph, the Atlanta Olympics bomber had connections to Missouri compounds that preach Christian Identity doctrines.

In searches of inmates and their property staff may come across Nazi symbols and paraphernalia, White Supremacist and Neo-Nazi propaganda such as *The Turner Diaries* or *88 Precepts* by David Lane. Neo-Nazi militants may use codes and ciphers in writings and correspondence and such terms as "Texas Republic" (corresponding to separatist denial of the annexation of Texas by the United States) "The 14 Words" (David Lane's 14 words of white nationalist defiance "We must secure the existence of our people and a future for White Children." and "14/88" or "1488" (which correspond to either the 14 Words or to the first and eighth letters of the alphabet, "AH" for Adolph Hitler) and the 88 Precepts of Lane, taken from the statement, 88 words in length, of Hitler in *Mein Kampf*, Volume 1, Chapter 8.

Important dates for these groups include April 19th (in 1775, the beginning of the American Revolution with the skirmishes at Lexington and Concord and the anniversary of both the Oklahoma City bombing and the fiery end of the Branch Davidian Waco, Texas standoff with the F.B.I.), and April 20th (Adolph Hitler's birthday and the anniversary of the Columbine, Colorado massacre). Members of a criminal gang may have some neo-Nazi or white supremacist beliefs. These are not necessarily violent criminal extremists. Remember that there are other far right violent or criminal extremist groups which may have nothing to do with white supremacist or Neo-Nazi doctrines. But whatever axe to grind that these loners or groups have, they all deny the legitimacy of the local, state and/or federal government and their powers and resort to violence or other criminal means to achieve their goals of political, social or religious change.

DO NOT CONCERN YOURSELF WITH CONSTITUTIONALLY PROTECTED BELIEFS AND SPEECH.

KEEP AN EYE OUT FOR DOMESTIC LONE WOLVES AND GROUPS THAT PARTICIPATE IN OR ACTIVELY SUPPORT VIOLENCE OR OTHER CRIMINAL MEANS TO ACHIEVE POLITICAL OR RELIGIOUS CHANGE &

NAZI PARAPHERNALIA AND SYMBOLS, CODES, CYPHERS AND DATES.

---

6 RADICALIZATION OF INMATES

In this chapter we discuss some possible signs of inmate radicalization. Remember that these signs do not necessarily apply to lone wolves. *Not all of the behaviors or manners of dress discussed are exclusive to radicals who are violent or criminal extremists.* Quick changes of group or individual behavior and/or manner of dress could be an indicator that radicalization has started, but *it could also be Constitutionally protected religious expression.* More investigation may be necessary to determine whether the behavioral changes are evidence of radicalization. Although we emphasize al-Qaida and like groups in this chapter, the radicalization of other violent or criminal extremists, whether of the far left or far right, is remarkably the same.

There are certain steps that inmates go through when becoming a violent or criminal extremist. Whether a domestic or international terrorist, these steps are similar. Remember that these stages may take place over a long period of time or quite quickly. In the case of homegrown converts, radicalization may come so quickly that they skip early stages or progress swiftly to action.

In the early stages, an inmate may feel alienated from or hurt by others. He may be protesting what he perceives to be an injustice. He might be seeking acceptance by trying to fit into the group or reinterpreting his religious faith.

This searching leads him to take further steps. He may become alienated from his family and former associates and now affiliates closely only with like-minded ones.

The group then indoctrinates the inmate. They may test his readiness to participate in jihad. He may be trained in paramilitary techniques and radical religious instruction.

Finally, the inmate acts through participation. He may commit an act of jihad or violent holy war or may recruit others to participate. He may support these acts through financing or facilitation in some sort of physical capacity.

We must remember, however, that those who have truly made the transition from conversion to jihad may change dress and behavior to <u>blend in and avoid detection.</u>

We might note the inmate's quick change from non-religious behavior to behaviors such as growing his beard long and perhaps shaving off his moustache. He may cut hair close to head. He may cut back his fingernails with no white showing. He might fold up the fringes of his pant legs just above the ankles. He may develop a small callous on the forehead from prayer and might have sudden weight loss due to fasting.

Other sudden changes we might note are tensions in the family, withdrawal from other inmates, extremely heated religious or political rhetoric, possession of jihadist literature or printouts from jihadist websites, an intense interest in the historical beginnings of Islam and an increase in aggressiveness toward inmates who do not share his beliefs and toward staff.

Still more sudden group changes we want to keep alert for are: the practicing of prayer oration as a group outside of the authorized chapel services, adventurous group activities, extreme resistance to group monitoring in the chapel and the exchanging of jihadist propaganda. The group acceptance of former criminals who have converted and the taking of measures of security to avoid monitoring by staff may also be indicators.

Be alert to swift changes in dress, grooming and behavior, one inmate or imam dictating this behavior, dress or grooming to others and attempts of groups to enact security procedures.

If you note any of the above signs in an individual inmate or a group of inmates, report your suspicions to investigative personnel immediately.

Remember that in order for terrorist cells to operate effectively, they need certain things, to include the ability to communicate with other prisoners, control over part of the prison, access to propaganda and training material, contact with other terrorist groups outside of the prison and/or the ability to corrupt prison or other government officials.

IF WE LIMIT AND CLOSELY SUPERVISE TERRORIST COMMUNICATIONS, IT IS VERY DIFFICULT FOR THEM TO ORGANIZE & RADICALIZE.

Some other signs to look out for: prisoners may attempt to separate from the general population and authorized chapel religious services to have their own meetings or they may even have unauthorized meetings to the side within otherwise authorized Islamic services and gatherings. They may attempt to engage in some sort of military drill, conduct martial arts training or attempt to receive altered Qurans with inserted inflammatory commentaries. They may smuggle jihadist materials in property when transferring to another facility or try to receive them through the mail.

A charismatic inmate may attempt to challenge or force out an authorized imam or other clergy. Change of the group's usual manner of dress or personal hygiene habits, such as ceremonial washing, may be indicators.

Imams or other employees, contractors or volunteers may try to have unauthorized communications with inmates. They may accept telephone calls from inmates . There may be a strong inmate or imam resistance to having appropriate staff present during group Islamic functions or monitoring.

There are some practices that we should adhere to so as to avoid an environment for radicalization, also. Do not use inmates as imams or religious leaders and fully vet all employees, volunteers and contractors.

Do not assign terrorist offenders as orderlies or clerks in the religious services areas. Have close supervision of all Islamic religious services.

To identify the inmate Islamic leaders, watch for who the Muslim prisoners go to for advice. Identify who gives the call for prayer and who leads the prayer. The leaders will generally follow institution the rules by the book so as to not draw attention to themselves.

Most cases of prison radicalization and recruitment tend to be originated by domestic extremists with little or no foreign connections. Some radicalized Islamic inmates are current or former members of street or prison gangs.

> *KEEP CLOSE SUPERVISION OF THE CHAPEL AND OTHER AREAS WHERE INMATES MAY GATHER IN GROUPS*
>
> *KEEP AN EYE OUT FOR CHANGES IN BEHAVIOR THAT MAY INDICATE RADICALIZATION.*
>
> *INFORM INVESTIGATIVE STAFF IMMEDIATELY OF ANY SUSPICIOUS ACTIVITY.*

7 GENERAL CHECKPOINT SAFETY

Corrections personnel with no military background may be unfamiliar with procedures regarding vehicle checkpoints. Likely, if a checkpoint has been manned, the institution's CEO has determined that there is a terrorist threat and has limited vehicular access to the institution grounds.

A vehicle checkpoint should have a barrier that can effectively stop vehicular traffic onto institution grounds unless authorized to enter. Those vehicles not authorized to enter should have a turn-around lane before reaching the barrier where vehicles are searched so that unauthorized vehicles are not allowed on the property.

At stages of high terrorism risk, more than one checkpoint, each with a barrier, should be layered so that if one checkpoint is breached, subsequent checkpoints can stop the intruder or slow the vehicle down enough to be intercepted by mobile response teams prior to reaching the inner vehicle barriers surrounding the target.

Checkpoints should have a <u>minimum</u> of three personnel assigned to them (preferably more): one for screening the visitor, and, if necessary, searching the vehicle, one for escorting the visitor to a visitor area and supervising the visitor until the search is complete and one for observing and protecting the entire checkpoint and operation of the barrier from a safe distance. These duties should be rotated frequently so that all personnel remain alert.

Officer #1 Duties: Be alert and observant of the driver as he approaches the checkpoint. Does he appear to know how to drive the vehicle well, or is he operating the vehicle like he is unfamiliar with it?

Be observant of the activity in the vehicle. Have it stop and the driver turn it off and remove the vehicle keys. Stand behind the driver and to the rear of the door. Do not allow the driver or occupants to exit the vehicle until instructed to do so.

Check photo identification thoroughly against the visitor. Ask detailed questions about the visitor's need to enter and his/her background.

Check the vehicle registration. If it is a delivery person, check the vehicle manifest and the driver log and make sure that the delivery is expected and authorized by the CEO.

Have the driver do something that only a regular driver would know how to do, such as turn on the overhead light or dash lights or to change the radio to your favorite station. Have the driver open all doors and hatches on the vehicle, as well as the hood and the trunk, if applicable.

Then have the driver go to the visitor waiting area with the #2 officer while the search is being completed. Visually check the exterior of the vehicle first, looking for suspicious wiring and devices underneath the vehicle, in the engine compartment, the cab, interior and trunk/cargo area. If you note any suspicious wiring or devices, immediately evacuate the area and have bomb technicians called to the scene. Do not attempt to move or disarm the device yourself, even if it seems to be a simple device.

Be alert for fresh, orange rust or liquid leaking from the cargo area, which could indicate a leaking bomb. Be alert for wiring or fuses running from the driver's seat to the rear seat, trunk or cargo area. Be alert for wiring running from one container to another and/or flammable gas cylinders or tanks in the rear seat, trunk or cargo area, which are used to enhance explosive effect.

Note: If the #1 Officer suspects that the driver or occupants are about to either engage him in small arms fire, detonate the VBIED at the checkpoint and/or attempt to breach the vehicle gate, his/her main duty is to protect him/herself. The #1 officer should warn his partners using a prearranged hand signal, evacuate beyond the 25-50 foot initial blast pressure area as soon as possible and find cover from shrapnel and debris. The farther he is away the better. If he is under fire, he should drop to make a smaller target and zigzag, finding cover. Any cover fire should be provided by the #3 officer.

Officer #2 Duties: Stand to the rear right side of the vehicle and back up the #1 officer while he is checking identification. Be observant of what is happening in the vehicle. Supervise any occupants and the driver at the visitor waiting area. Instruct them not to place their hands in their pockets or coats and not to use cell phones or any other device. When the #1 officer states that the vehicle is clear, escort the visitor(s) back to the vehicle. If under attack, he should clear the initial blast pressure area and find cover prior to returning fire.

Officer #3 Duties: Man a post with cover that can observe the entire checkpoint from a safe distance, preferably at least 50 ft. behind the barrier, vehicle search area and visitor supervision area. Operate the vehicle barrier gate when the #1 Officer informs you that the vehicle is clear by pre-arranged hand signal.

Know how to operate the kill switch for the vehicle barrier and be ready to do so instantly in an attack. Be ready to provide cover fire to protect the #1 and #2 officer in an attack. Immediately radio the dispatcher and other layered checkpoints in the event of an attack.

Vehicle Barrier Kill Switch: There should be a kill switch at each automatic gate that disables the vehicle gate in case of an armed attack. If a post is overwhelmed, such a kill switch could slow down attackers long enough for response forces to thwart them.

Layered Perimeter Security: There should be more layered perimeter security than simply vehicle checkpoints when there is a high risk of terrorist attack. The use of mobile patrols and multiple response forces is advisable, as well as towers, if available (see below). A primary reason for checkpoint security is to slow down an attacker so that response forces can arrive in time to stop acquisition of the target.

Towers and Layered Security: In the Middle East, heavily secured towers are used both for observation and for perimeter defense. These towers are protected by layers of anti-vehicle and anti-personnel barriers to make them difficult to attack. If towers are available, it would be wise to reinforce their security and use them as an inner layer of defense in case of threat of terrorist attack.

An example of good use of towers was the Saudi Arabian oil processing facility attack in 2006. When suicide bombers had successfully breached an outer checkpoint of the facility, armed defenders from two such observation towers were able to stop the attackers before they were able to reach their target.

The checkpoint personnel on the outermost layers should be the best trained anti terrorism professionals. If a terrorist is detected early at a checkpoint in the outer layers, this could mitigate a terrorist attack.

In the next chapter, we will examine general explosives safety.

8 GENERAL EXPLOSIVES SAFETY

By far, most terrorist-related injuries involve the use of explosives. Improvised explosive devices (IEDs) are used most frequently today. Vehicle-borne IEDs (VBIEDs) are a very popular device used by violent criminal extremists. In the Middle East and South Asia, stationary VBIEDs are used to ambush targets and mobile VBIEDs are used to breach and bypass physical security barriers or access control points, and to attack targets. The use of suicide bombers is prevalent among radical Islamic militant groups such as al-Qaida, Hezbollah, Palestinian Islamic Jihad, Hamas and others. Defending against this potential domestic threat is a great challenge to U.S. law enforcement personnel.

The Basic Life or Death Facts

Spend the least amount of time possible in the immediate area of a suspicious device. Avoid this exclusion zone totally if possible. If you must enter it (only due to immediate concerns such as wounded victims or fire containment), quickly use hit and run tactics (go in, accomplish a single objective with a limited number of responders and quickly get out).

Stay as far away from the suspicious device as possible , warn others and keep them as far away as possible.

Take appropriate cover and use personal protective equipment. Do not allow those without authorization of the incident commander or without appropriate personal protective equipment to enter the exclusion zone around the suspicious device or blast site.

Your foremost concerns as a responder on the scene are:

#1: Life & Safety

YOUR LIFE COMES FIRST! Don't run into a deadly trap. Terrorists use two or more explosives to lure first responders in. You are no help to anyone as a responder if you are dead or wounded. Have a small team do a quick extraction of the victims and bring them to an area outside of the exclusion zone for triage and first aid treatment. If the victims can walk out, they should be instructed to do so. Remember that the victims may be deaf and/or stunned from the blast. Use hand signals. Evacuate bystanders, contain the fire and have a team quickly search for other suspicious devices in the general area, especially routes used for evacuation.

#2: Security

Security should be multi-layered. Restrict all vehicle and foot traffic into the response zones. Have a safe staging area away from the incident for responders that has been searched and deemed safe. Only bring in responders that are immediately needed to secure the scene and conduct emergency operations at hand. Remember that this may just be a diversion for another attack. Terrorists may be planning to bring in a second IED or VBIED to inflict more casualties.

#3: Evidence Preservation

Even the slightest piece of evidence that appears as trash around the scene could lead investigators to the perpetrator(s). The explosive device is still there. It is just in a myriad of pieces waiting to be documented and put back together again. Only allow as many personnel into the area as the situation warrants and instruct them to leave everything where it lies except the wounded. Do not allow unauthorized or unnecessary people on the scene.

MAIL BOMBS AND HAZARDOUS MAILINGS

Most mail bombs are sent to the target's home, not the place of his or her employment. Mail is thoroughly screened at correctional facilities, but there is always the possibility that a hazardous mailing or mail bomb could get through screening. We should thoroughly train mail room staff in detection of these devices and terrorist contraband. What are some signs you should be alert for?

IS THE ADDRESS TYPED OR WRITTEN IN BLOCK LETTERS?

IS IT ADDRESSED TO A TITLE?

IS THE ADDRESS INCORRECT OR MISSPELLED?

IS THERE NO RETURN ADDRESS OR A FAKE RETURN ADDRESS?

DOES THE POSTMARK MATCH THE RETURN ADDRESS?

IS THE MAIL FROM A FOREIGN COUNTRY, DOES IT HAVE TOO MUCH POSTAGE OR IS IT PRE-POSTED?

IS THE MAILING OVERLY-SEALED?

IS THE ENVELOPE OVER 1/10" THICK & NOT BENDABLE?

IF A PACKAGE, IS THE WRAPPING SLOPPILY DONE?

IS THE PACKAGE WEIGHT UNEVENLY DISTRIBUTED?

ARE THERE WIRES PROTRUDING OR ANY OILY STAINS?

DOES THE MAILING SMELL STRANGELY?

These could be some indicators of a mail bomb or hazardous mailing. Do not try to open up a suspicious package. Evacuate and secure the area. Try to leave a 4 foot wide path from the bomb to the door to allow a robot to get to it. If in the institution, contact the supervisor. If at home, contact local police. If a hazardous mailing is suspected, turn off all HVAC systems and fans, secure the area, isolate all affected to avoid cross-contamination and seek medical aid immediately.

EXPLOSIVES ATTACK SAFETY

Israeli and secular Muslim governments have used the layered security approach to thwart suicide bombers and armed assaults. This involves several layers of security (the outermost layer being intelligence gathering) to slow and stop a bomber or attacker before he/she reaches a likely target and to mitigate the effects of an attack. The more layers, the more chance there is of stopping an attacker from reaching the target.

Vehicular traffic around a potential target should be controlled by the use of checkpoints and vehicle barriers. Effective barriers should be used around likely targets to prevent a vehicle from entering the minimum safe bomb distance from the building without authorization. Vehicles should be slowed down by various techniques so that these barriers cannot be normally breached.

A bomb, when detonated, poses a number of dangers to surrounding personnel in addition to fire and heat. First, an over-pressure blast wave is created which will crush or propel anything in its path for a certain distance around the bomb, the exact distance depending upon the explosive capacity and location of the bomb and surrounding terrain and buildings. Even a fairly large bomb that is detonated out-of-doors will have its over-pressure wave start quickly dissipating by about four car lengths and then will further gradually and exponentially dissipate beyond this distance.

Personnel should make every effort to immediately get out of this 25-to-50 foot over-pressure blast wave area surrounding the bomb. This will increase your chances of survival. However, it must be remembered that this blast wave can "skip" over the ground, like a rock that is skipped upon a body of water. The blast wave can also reflect off of buildings and other sturdy structures, like a billiard ball bouncing off of a bumper, potentially resulting in beyond-line-of-sight, remote areas being affected outside of the initial blast area .

A second danger to surrounding personnel and structures is the immediate vacuum (or reverse pressure) created by the air being quickly sucked out of this initial over-pressure blast area. If the bomb has enough explosive capacity and is very close to, inside of, or underneath a building (in the case of a parking garage or basement) when the explosion occurs, it can stress building supports in the opposite direction, causing the building to collapse.

A third danger, especially in the open, is shrapnel from the bomb and debris from surrounding objects, which can greatly outdistance the initial blast over-pressure wave and cause deadly injuries. As much space should be placed between the bomb and personnel as possible, and if immediate detonation is expected, personnel should seek cover from shrapnel and debris as soon as the 25-50 foot initial over-pressure wave area is cleared. Personnel inside of a building should also seek cover as far away from the bomb as possible from flying window glass, debris and shrapnel. If the bomb detonation is imminent it may be better to keep occupants in the opposite side of the building, using it as a buffer. Remember, however, that the closer the bomb is to the building, the more dangerous it is.

MODERN TERRORIST I.E.D. TACTICS

Assault Teams

Radical Islamic terrorist groups in the Middle East increasingly use armed assault teams to eliminate armed guards prior to a VBIED attack. In an al-Qaida attack on an oil facility in Saudi Arabia, an armed team was positioned beyond the exterior of an outermost perimeter gate to give small arms cover fire to two VBIEDs using trucks disguised as authorized vehicles. The first VBIED destroyed the checkpoint and gate. The second VBIED entered the secure perimeter but was immediately stopped by armed guards in perimeter towers, foiling the attack.

Double-tap

Double-tap is the use of two explosive devices in succession. This method was first used successfully by the IRA. It has been adopted by al-Qaida, Hezbollah, Hamas, Palestinian Islamic Jihad and other radical Islamic groups. It has also been used by domestic terror bombers such as Eric Rudolph. The second bomb is detonated in the same area as the first bomb to target first responders who gather into the area and/or to target the evacuation route of survivors for a greater sense of panic and higher casualty rate. The second bomb can also target bomb technicians attempting to defuse or detonate the first bomb. First responders should quickly set up multi-layered perimeter security around the site to prevent a second person and/or vehicle from attacking with a second bomb. They should also immediately search all surrounding areas for hidden secondary devices.

Triple-tap

Triple-tap is the use of three explosive devices in succession. This method was seen in Baghdad, Iraq, where, at the perimeter of the Palestine Hotel, the first VBIED was used to make a gap in a perimeter blast wall. Then a second VBIED was used to destroy an Iraqi security force checkpoint. A few minutes later a third, significantly larger VBIED was then driven through the breached checkpoint and the breached blast wall in an attempt to attack the target, foreigners lodged at the Palestine Hotel. The last VBIED was stopped by blast debris and response personnel and it detonated prematurely.

A lesson gleaned: Terrorists may use the first VBIEDs to breach physical security barriers such as gates, fences, blast walls and other vehicle barriers. They may also be used to neutralize armed guards at checkpoints so that a larger VBIED can proceed to the target.

HAVE WELL-TRAINED COUNTERTERRORISM PERSONNEL IN THE MAIL ROOM AND ON PERIMETER POSTS.

TIME, DISTANCE AND SHIELDING CAN SAVE YOUR LIFE AND OTHERS IN AN EXPLOSIVES INCIDENT.

USE SECURITY LAYERING.

BEWARE OF MULTIPLE BOMBS OR BOMBERS.

YOUR IMMEDIATE PRIORITIES ARE LIFE SAFETY, SECURITY AND EVIDENCE PRESERVATION.

9 GENERAL VIOLENT EXTREMISM ORGANIZATION AND TACTICS

Terrorists and Their Worldview

Terrorist organizations are made up of individuals. Just as no two individuals are exactly alike, no two terrorists are exactly alike. Each terrorist has his own unique personality. He also has a view of the world around him, usually dictated by the ideology of the group he belongs to. Understanding a terrorist means getting into his or her mind. It is the first step to successfully countering terrorist activities in prison.

There is much misunderstanding in the Western world about the nature of al-Qaida. Al-Qaida is really two things. Core al-Qaida is a small, but very real, clandestine, cellular organization that is based in the tribal areas of northwest Pakistan. It is a global network that recruits people of all races, creeds and religious backgrounds. Yet, with globalization and the advent of the internet, al-Qaida has also become a force for spreading propaganda and training materials to encourage other like-minded individuals to take up arms in its cause, the establishment of an Islamic caliphate under sharia law by force.

Put yourself into the mind of a core al-Qaida operative. Think like him. You sincerely believe that you are a soldier fighting a divine war against unbelievers. You believe that you are an agent of God. Do you feel empowered? Justified in your course? You are a part of a brotherhood. If pressured to betray a brother, will you do it easily, knowingly?

As you can imagine, it is very difficult, if not impossible, to infiltrate a core al-Qaida network. It could take many years. It may be easier to infiltrate a homegrown terrorist cell once identified, however. Homegrown terrorists are those who may have contact with core al-Qaida beliefs, usually through the internet or contact with religious radicals. But, unlike a core al-Qaida cell, they are self-indoctrinating, self-training, and financially self-sustaining. These groups are very difficult to detect through normal intelligence gathering techniques because they may form quickly. How can we detect a terrorist network or cell within the prison environment? One way is by knowing the dynamics of an al-Qaida cell, which are found in al-Qaida training manuals published on the internet.

Signs of Terrorists in Prison

Al-Qaida and like group members do not stop being terrorists simply because they are placed in prison. They continue to organize into networks. It was reported that, upon arrival at Camp Delta in Guantanamo Bay, captured terrorist operatives organized according to the Manchester, England "Al Qaeda Manual" that was introduced into the New York trial of the East African embassy bombers. What are some of the highlights of this and other terrorist how-to manuals?

The network is usually made up of members that take on different roles. As you observe inmate and staff interactions within the institution, do you note any that are taking on similar characteristics?

Remember that homegrown cells may not take on all the characteristics of a core al-Qaida cell. Yet a hybrid supportive social network will still exist. There may also be some similarities with criminal gang structures. But while a terrorist cell may use criminal activities to its own ends (perhaps for fund raising, acquirement of supplies or control of areas), its objective is a politico-socio-religious one. Its methods and outcomes are more brutal and may involve mass casualties. The following is simply a general description of a terrorist network. These are not titles.

The operations leader:

The leader is intensely devoted to his beliefs. He is usually an inmate who does not wish to stand out to staff. He will abide by institution rules. He has appointed other cell members to perform as deputies to accomplish network operations and support.

The religious leader:

The imam, or clergyman, is responsible for keeping up the spirituality of "brothers" belonging to the network. In the stages just prior to and after the attacks of September 11th, it was customary for radical imams and their followers to force out moderate imams from established religious services. With increased monitoring after these attacks, however, radical spiritual activities are more likely to be done covertly, separate from authorized religious meetings. This imam may use unauthorized radical Islamic materials or Qurans with inserted inflammatory statements.

The welfare attendant:

The network is made up of "brothers" that look after each other's welfare. All material goods received by members are collected and given to this welfare attendant, whose job is the fair and equal distribution of the goods to other network members.

The morale officer:

Members of the network could be easily discouraged and their morale broken in a prison environment. The morale officer organizes the recreational and leisure activities of the network members to encourage them to hang on to their beliefs and the brotherhood.

The medic:

There may be a network member assigned to look to the medical needs of the brothers in the cell.

The liaison officer:

Only one member of the network is allowed to interact and communicate with prison staff in behalf of the network. The liaison officer is appointed by the leader to take on this role.

The mail men:

The network must continue to communicate with other members in and outside of prison. Many mail men or "freedom transmitters" may make up this communication system to get messages into and out of the institution. Prison staff may even take on a role, wittingly or unwittingly, in this communication.

The greeter(s):

Prospective members are carefully screened, indoctrinated, trained, and kept separate from other members of the network until they are thoroughly vetted. They are usually admitted into the network just before an operation.

The person appointed as a greeter is the "handler" for each prospective recruit to accomplish this. He will be covert, perhaps closely watching new

Islamic inmates at *bona fide* institutional chapel meetings and elsewhere to ascertain whether they are potential recruits. Then the greeter may take the recruit aside, meeting with him outside of chapel meetings. He may start with non-religious conversation to build up a rapport. Then he may gently probe for common sympathies. If he finds such, he will attempt to introduce propaganda of the group. Gradually the recruit may become radicalized.

Recruits from the United States or elsewhere in the West who are ignorant of the Quran in Arabic tend to radicalize much more quickly than those brought up in a predominantly Muslim country. If the westerner is radicalized, he may tend to be even more zealous than his counterpart overseas. The greeter may have a much harder time trying to radicalize one who has been immersed in moderate Islam all his life and who has a foundation of knowledge about the Quran untainted by al-Qaida rhetoric.

The foot soldiers:

A foot soldier may be recruited for a specific task or mission, such as a suicide attack. The handler will stay with this individual throughout his indoctrination and training, perhaps even accompanying him to a place just outside the attack area to monitor the attack and ensure that the foot soldier does not abort it. He may have a wireless trigger which he will engage if the recruit gets caught or if he tries to back out of the operation.

The operations support specialists:

Some members are specially trained in weapons or explosives. They are used to design and build devices used in an attack. They may be called upon to train the individual foot soldier that actually uses the device in an attack. Common titles of bomb makers include "The Engineer" or "The Chemist". Many times explosives will have secondary means of detonation, such as a dead man's trigger or a remote held by the handler.

What if you detect activity such as this? What should you do?

Do not let the suspicious acting inmate, volunteer, contractor or employee know that you have detected the activity. Immediately and confidentially contact your investigative personnel before taking action. It may be deemed that more surveillance is necessary to reveal the entire network and its operation and to gather evidence for future prosecution in court.

What should you be on the lookout for as a prison employee?

Al-Qaida and like terrorists plan meticulously for attacks. Watch for these signs of possible terrorist activity:

Surveillance:

Are there unauthorized individuals on the institution property or staff members, volunteers or contractors in areas where they are not authorized to be? Are they using webcams, cell cams or any other recording or photographic equipment? Are they drawing sketches or taking notes?

Suspicious Questioning:

Are unauthorized persons questioning you about information pertaining to security, schedules or other pertinent information they are not entitled to? Remember to never give out sensitive information to those you have not verified as authorized or to speak to others about sensitive information in public places. Also, remember that core al-Qaida operatives and those of their franchise affiliates have been instructed to infiltrate targets to gain information. Report any suspicions immediately.

Tests of Security:

Terrorists may probe, or test security to learn procedures and to ascertain their parameters of movement. They may also try to come on the property often to establish familiarity with corrections staff, who come to view their presence as "normal".

Acquiring Supplies:

In your searches of inmates and their areas, have you detected a stockpile of supplies or ingredients that could be used in an attack or an escape?

Suspicious People Who Do Not Belong:

Are persons who are behaving in a manner that just doesn't seem right on or near the property? Many times our neighbors are our best eyes and ears. Build a rapport with locals and encourage them to report any suspicious activity.

Dry Run or Trial Run:

Terrorists have been known to do a "dress rehearsal" just
prior to an attack. They travel to and may come on the property and travel
to points where they will operate in an attack. But they will not possess
weapons or explosives so as not to arouse suspicion if caught. This is why it
is imperative to thoroughly investigate and document trespassers, even if
they seem at first glance to be innocent. Always be cautious when
investigating these individuals. This may not be a trial run; this may be an
attack.

Getting Into Position:

Terrorist assets must be placed into position before an attack can take
place. This may be our last chance to stop it before it occurs or mitigate it.

Do groups of people get dropped off together, yet then start acting as if
they do not know each other?

Does one vehicle park, the driver get out, and get whisked off by another
vehicle?

Does a person place a suspicious object in a public area such as a backpack
or duffel bag and then leave, as the two Boston Marathon bombers and
Eric Rudolph did? If so, an attack may be in progress. Report it and use
extreme caution. Stay away from suspicious bags and warn others to stay
away from them.

Terrorist Attack Cell Tactics Against Hard Targets

How to Storm a Prison is a very real terrorist training document found on the
open internet. Violent extremists have used its principles repeatedly to
penetrate the hardest targets where their prisoners are housed in
Afghanistan and Pakistan. The very headquarters of the Afghan Prison
system was successfully attacked using some of these methods! We will
briefly examine them.

Pre-operational Surveillance Teams

Terrorists may use intelligence cells separate from the attack cell to gain information by examining the target's surroundings. They may take pictures of the target and the surrounding areas, taking special note of details about the guard system and its response to intrusions. They conduct surveillance of roads that lead to the prison and of the best routes for approaching it, taking note of the nearest cover, the best timing and the best apparel for the attack. This unit is generally not armed, but use caution!

This surveillance team may try to note the length of time for one guard shift, the time of the changing of the guard, the location of guard stations and the individual guards' habits during their shift, the weather conditions, the number of ammunition rounds, the type of weapons, the equipment and the vehicles available to the guard force. They will note the main road and secondary roads leading to the target: their width, their length, pavement conditions, traffic, buildings and the location of police stations. They may travel at different times of day and night from the target to the extraction points. It is their job to gather all the necessary information for the completion of the operation.

Attack Cells

Multiple groups or cells, may be used to conduct a comprehensive assault on a correctional facility. They may inform terrorist prisoners that the operation is planned. They may release large numbers of prisoners during the attack to create confusion.

The cells will also focus on their exiting route if escape or hit and run assault is their goal. This may simply be an action to intimidate prison staff and the local populace and to show support for the prisoners.

Terrorists are told to train, train, train. Their training includes the silent killing of guards on posts. They have been trained proficiently in explosives and arson methods. They may employ prison vehicles, wear uniforms of the police or local civilian clothing. They may practice using police radios, speaking the language of the community and communicating in code. They may practice storming gates and rooms and disabling towers.

These cell members may practice working in small, totally separate groups without central leadership in case their leaders are neutralized. They may train in techniques to surprise, deceive and draw away the security forces from the real objective or penetration point.

Planning the Assault

Cells may make multiple penetrations through the outer perimeter. They may bypass the greatest security on the main gate or other main areas. They will be ready to penetrate any lock and may set off explosions in many different places to confuse the guards. They are specifically instructed to kill the guards in towers quietly.

They are told that the best time to attack is at the end of the day. They believe that it will be unexpected and that they will be able to disappear into the darkness of night.

Multiple cells may have different and separate objectives:

The information cell (surveillance and reconnaissance)

The equipment and transportation cells (obtains and creates documents, devices, vehicles, safe house equipment, transports escapees and protects them upon arrival at the safe house after escape).

The execution or attack cell (storms the prison, explosives detonation and direction of escapees---they may be in correctional uniforms of the facility)

The protection cell (covers all the operational groups from first responders)

The initial entry clearing cell (targets the guards on the perimeter)

The reserve cell (waits in case any cell needs reinforcement or replacement and is trained to take over the duties of each cell)

As corrections staff at the scene of a major attack we must keep in the back of our minds that there may be more cells involved than just the attack cell that has been detected. Remember, all groups above with the possible exception of the information cell may have military grade weaponry and explosives.

When terrorists attack a prisoner transport

Their primary goal is to separate the other guard vehicles from the prisoner vehicle and eliminate them. Prior to the attempt they may try to obtain information about the types of prisoner vehicles normally used and the number and locations of guards, prisoners, locks and chains.

Just as with the attack on a prison, several cells may be used, one to attack and neutralize the guard vehicle(s), one to storm the prisoner transport vehicle, one to protect the entire operation from responders, one that receives the repatriated prisoners and transports them to the safe house and one reserve group to back up cells as needed. There may be a recon group that gives advance warning of approaching first responders.

Do these sound like military operations to you? The fact is, terrorists many times even quote the opponents' military technical manuals in their own!

Prison personnel must instantly change from a law enforcement mode to a counterterrorism defensive mode when an attack occurs. Remember that core al-Qaida and like operatives believe that they are soldiers in a divine war and they will attack civilian law enforcement and corrections with military tactics and weaponry. The most dangerous groups will not take any law enforcement officer alive. Others may be gathered as hostages if cornered. They will kill all publicly for media attention. In <u>every</u> scenario of al-Qaida training videos found in Afghanistan the hostages were killed.

Likely, the very first responders to the incident are the only ones that will be able to thwart a surprise terrorist attack. There will be no time to form the special operations teams. It will start and then soon thereafter it will be over, whatever happens. Will you be dead or will you be alive?

<u>Do not give up, even if wounded</u>. The terrorist has one goal: to kill you, even if you surrender! <u>Keep the attackers engaged</u> and resist all you can! Slow their attack and try your best to <u>prevent barricading</u>. Remember that <u>you are the hostages' only hope</u>. If you hold out, other staff may arrive in support. Do not allow your force to be distracted by diversions in another area.

What you can do as a guard or responder

Be wary of uniformed attackers and first responders you do not know. identify and search all first responders. This first attack may be just a diversion. The main attack may be coming through this breach of the perimeter. Shore up the security breach immediately. Remember that the main attack may occur somewhere else on the property.

Set up multi-layered security around the target as soon as possible. The more rings, or layers of security the better your chances to stop or slow down a second or third attempt to breach the perimeter or the next layer. Keep multiple armed mobile reserve groups in case of diversions.

Maintain good communication with responders. Use simple language so that staff from other agencies and those who have no counterterrorism training will understand you.

Encircle and/or contain the attack as soon as possible. Have strike teams searching for and apprehending support cells in the surrounding area.

If you are a potential first responder and/or incident commander:

Knowledge is power. Know your adversaries.

Gain the right mindset well before the attack begins.

Get as much training and education as you can in counterterrorism.

Train with those who will be responding with you, build a rapport with other agencies in your local area and let them know what you will be doing in a terrorist attack. Do hands on, realistic training with those agencies that will be responding if terrorists attack.

Know the area you will defend and environmental factors such as buildings, structures and terrain.

Know your terrorist inmates. Gain intelligence from them, their communications and their associates. Search them and their cells frequently for intelligence information and contraband. Use inmate informants well.

Make sure that those you supervise are well trained in counterterrorism techniques in an emergency. Remember that any one of them could be an incident commander if they are the first one on the scene.

Do your best to be a first Preventer so you don't have to be a first responder.

> *COULD __YOU__ EFFECTIVELY EXECUTE INCIDENT COMMANDER RESPONSIBILITIES IF FIRST ON SCENE?*
>
> *DO YOU KNOW THE SIGNS OF TERRORISM SO YOU CAN PREVENT AN ATTACK RATHER THAN RESPOND TO ONE?*

10 THE FUTURE OF EXTREMISM AND YOU

According to current trends, future acts of violent extremism in the United States are likely to be committed by lone individuals or homegrown terrorist groups with little or no connection to international groups. However, core al-Qaida and al-Qaida franchise groups are still trying hard to infiltrate and attack the United States. They seek to recruit those who hold Western passports and who fit into American society.

Yet we in the counterterrorism community are not prophets or soothsayers. We really do not know what the future holds as far as new causes for terrorists to promote, new groups that may form and new tactics that may be employed. We must remain vigilant, monitor worldwide trends and be ready to adapt and be proactive as to emerging and growing threats.

Terrorism in the 21st century has become one of the greatest challenges facing corrections in the United States. Rise up to meet this challenge.

Continually train and re-train yourself and your staff in identification of ever-changing terrorist groups and their tactics. Conduct realistic exercises with your local agencies that will be first responders in a terrorism crisis.

Cooperate with other government agencies tasked to keep the nation safe and secure. Take advantage of the Correctional Intelligence Initiative (C.I.I.) for terrorism intelligence sharing. Work closely with the F.B.I. Joint Terrorism Task Force (J.T.T.F.) for your region and with your state fusion center.

Could You Be a Target?

The British call the period of the Irish Republican Army conflict the "Troubles." Many prison officials were targets of violence on and off duty. This is our time of "troubles". And long after al-Qaida ceases to exist, die-hard adherents will still be incarcerated in civilian correctional institutions and will still have the same dangerous worldview.

Whether you deem it likely or not that you could be attacked or kidnapped, law enforcement and corrections personnel are still considered by core al-Qaida and like terrorists to be soldiers in the opposing army in their war of "good versus evil". At the very least, you could be a target of outside or inside monitoring to gather intelligence about terrorist inmates and the security of the institution. You could also be a target of manipulation by "freedom transmitters" to get unmonitored communications to other terrorists in and outside of the institution. Corrections staff must be alert at all times for suspicious activity and immediately contact investigative personnel verbally and in writing. Remember that staff may be terrorists!

Think out of the box. Be realistic about potential threats and consider how to use the resources available to you to meet these threats. Be always thinking of "what if a terrorist did this or that...what would I do?" Go over your own scenarios and responses in your mind. Talk to your colleagues about counterterrorism. Don't be content with this resource or the training at your correctional facility. Pursue further training in counterterrorism outside your agency and keep abreast of the changing threat.

Remember the Lesson of Maze:

The world changed forever on September 11, 2001. Stay alert. Stay informed. Do not become complacent. All corrections staff, no matter what position held in the prison, must be anti-terrorism officers. It may mean your life and the lives of those around you one "quiet" day.

---

1. **WHAT DID THE EXTREMIST PRISONERS AT MAZE DO TO PREPARE FOR THEIR ESCAPE AND WHAT WERE THE RESULTS?**

2. **HOW DO EXTREMISM & CRIMINAL GANG MEMBERSHIP DIFFER?**

3. **WHAT SECURITY PROCEDURES CAN PREVENT OR MITIGATE ATTACKS?**

4. **LIST 4 CHARACTERISTICS OF A TERRORIST NETWORK IN PRISON.**

5. **LIST 4 INDICATORS OF INMATE RADICALIZATION.**

6. **WHAT ARE TWO TERRORIST I.E.D. TACTICS?**

7. **WHAT ARE TERRORIST TACTICS WHEN ATTACKING A PRISON?**

RECOMMENDED SOURCES OF FREE ANTI-TERRORISM INFORMATION AND TRAINING FOR LAW ENFORCEMENT AND CORRECTIONS EMPLOYEES:

THE STATE AND LOCAL ANTI-TERRORISM TRAINING (SLATT) PROGRAM

https://www.slatt.org/

THE UNITED STATES DEPARTMENT OF HOMELAND SECURITY'S TECHNICAL RESOURCE FOR INCIDENT PREVENTION (TRIPwire)

https://tripwire.dhs.gov/

THE FEDERAL EMERGENCY MANAGEMENT AGENCY'S NATIONAL PREPAREDNESS DIRECTORATE

http://www.training.fema.gov/

THE COMBATING TERRORISM CENTER AT WEST POINT

http://www.ctc.usma.edu/

THE NAVAL POSTGRADUATE SCHOOL, CENTER FOR HOMELAND DEFENSE AND SECURITY

https://www.chds.us/

References

Jason Burke, *Al Qaeda: Casting A Shadow of Terror*, 2003

Central Intelligence Agency, *Terrorists: Recruiting and Operating Behind Bars*
http://www.thesmokinggun.com/documents/crime/coming-prison-near-you

Jim Challis, *The Northern Ireland Prison Service 1920-1990 A History*, 1999

The Combating Terrorism Center at West Point, *The Encyclopedia of Jihad* (English Translation)

Federal Bureau of Investigation, "Preventing Terrorist Attacks, How You Can Help"

http://www.fbi.gov/about-us/investigate/terrorism/help-prevent-terrorist-attacks

Javier Jordan and Fernando Mañas, *External Signs of Radicalization and Jihadist Militancy*

http://www.academia.edu/2324655/External_signs_of_radicalization_and_jihadist_militancy

Memri TV, "Al-Qaeda Leader Ayman Al-Zawahiri's Interview to Al-Sahab (Part IV)", English translation, 2005

U.S. Department of Homeland Security, TRIPwire,
How to Storm a Prison (English translation)

U.S. Department of Justice, *Al Qaeda Manual* (confiscated by British police in Manchester, England)
http://www.usdoj.gov/ag/manualpart1_1.pdf
http://www.usdoj.gov/ag/manualpart1_2.pdf
http://www.usdoj.gov/ag/manualpart1_3.pdf
http://www.usdoj.gov/ag/manualpart1_4.pdf

ABOUT THE AUTHOR

Eric M. Vogt retired as a law enforcement officer and educator in 2011 from the United States Department of Justice, Federal Bureau of Prisons with 24 years of service. For his last six years of federal service he was assigned as a counterterrorism instructor. Eric trained several hundred law enforcement, corrections officers and support staff in southwest Missouri.

He is certified in homeland security at its highest level by the American Board for Certification in Homeland Security. Eric is the author of the journal article "Terrorists in Prison: The Challenge Facing Corrections" (*Inside Homeland Security*, Fall 2007 issue).

Eric is a veteran of the United States Army Military Police Corps. He was awarded a bachelor's degree in Justice and Law Administration by Western Connecticut State University, *cum laude*.

He is a member of the International Corrections and Prisons Association (ICPA), the Federal Law Enforcement Officers Association (FLEOA) and the American College of Forensic Examiners Institute (ACFEI).

Eric was a guest speaker at the annual conferences of ACFEI in 2007 and 2011 on the subject of prison counterterrorism issues. He currently resides in Missouri.

Made in the USA
Lexington, KY
05 June 2013